C++ Programming
Professional Made Easy
Sam Key

Expert C++ Programming
Language Success in a Day for
Any Computer User!
3rd Edition

Table Of Contents

Introduction

I want to thank you and congratulate you for purchasing the book, *"Professional C++ Programming Made Easy"*.

This book contains proven steps and strategies on how to learn the C++ programming language as well as its applications.

There's no need to be a professional developer to code quick and simple C++ programs. With this book, anyone with basic computer knowledge can explore and enjoy the power of the *C++ Programming Language*. Included are the following fundamental topics for any beginner to start coding *today:*

- The basic C++ terms

- Understanding the C++ Program Structure

- Working with Variables, Expressions, and Operators

- Using the Input and Output Stream for User Interaction

- Creating Logical Comparisons

- Creating Loops and Using Condition Statements

- Using Flow Control Statements

- Utilizing Multiple Functions and Passing Arguments

- Working with Arrays

- Using Pointers and Passing by Reference

- General Tips on Writing a Program

- Character Sequences

- Classes

- Friends and Inheritance

- And Many More!

Thanks again for purchasing this book, I hope you enjoy it!

Chapter 1 – Introduction to C++

What You Will Learn:

**A Brief History of the C++ Language

**C++ Basic Terminology

**C++ Program Structure

C++ is one of the most popular programming languages that people are using today. More specifically, C++ is a library of "commands" that tell your computer what to do and how to do it. These commands make up the *C++ source code.*

Take note that C++ is different from the *C* programming language that came before it. In fact, it is supposedly better version of the C language when *Bjarne Stroustrup* created it back in 1983.

Even today, the C++ language serves as the "starting point" for many experts in the world of programming. Although it is particularly easy to learn and apply, the ceiling for C++ mastery is incredibly high.

A Brief History of the C++ Language

The C++ programming languages goes way back to the 1970s. It was created by Bjarne Stroustrup, a Danish computer scientist, in 1979. His motivation for developing the language came from his experience in programming and work on his Ph.D. thesis. He worked with the Simula 67 language, which was considered as the first ever language to support object-oriented programming. He learned that Simula had highly helpful features for software development, but it was too slow for practical use. BCPL, on the other hand, was fast yet too low-level for large software development.

Eventually, Stroustrup worked at the Bell Laboratories, which was then known as AT&T Bell Laboratories. However, he had trouble analyzing the UNIX kernel in regard to distributed computing. Because of this, he tried to improve the C language by incorporating features similar to that of Simula. He chose C due to its portability, speed, and reliability. He also used a variety of other languages, including Ada, ML, ALGOL 68, and CLU for C++.

When he started to work on *C with Classes*, his main purpose was for it to be a superset of C. He wanted to incorporate object-oriented programming into the language. To this day, the C language is still renowned for its portability and functionality. Despite being portable, it does not sacrifice speed. Initially, Stroustrup added classes, strong typing, default argument, and inlining features to C.

He created Cfront, the first ever *C with Classes* compiler that was derived from CPre, a C language compiler. Cfront was designed to convert *C with Classes* codes to regular C. It was actually a self-hosting compiler because it was mostly written in *C with Classes*. This means that it has the ability to compile itself. This compiler has been a huge influence on future compilers as well as the Unix operating system. Unfortunately, integrating additional features to it proved to be difficult, which is why it was abandoned in 1993.

In 1983, *C with Classes* was changed to C++. Stroustrup adapted the operator ++ from the C language due to its purpose of incrementing variables. He added more features to it, including function overloading, virtual functions, const, and references that use &. In 1985, The C++ Programming was published and C++ was introduced to the commercial market. In 1989, C++ was updated and static and protected members and inheritance from classes were included.

In 1990, Borland Software Corporation released Turbo C++, a computer language and an integrated developmental environment. It paved the way for libraries that have had a significant influence on the development of C++. In the same year, The Annotated C++ Reference Manual was also released.

In 1998, C++ 98 was introduced. This standard had some problems, which were later addressed and revised in 2003. It was later called C++ 03. Two years later, the C++ standards committee filed a technical report that contains details on the multiple features that they planned to include in the most recent C++ standard. This new standard was called C++ 0x and was expected to be launched before 2010. However, it was only in 2011 when it was released.

In 2011, C++ 11 was released. Boost, a set of libraries for C++, made a substantial impact on this standard. Several modules were even directly derived from their libraries. In 2014, C++ 14 was launched as an extension to C++ 11. It featured several improvements and bug fixes. Its main purpose was to do what C++ 03 did to C++ 08. C++ 17, a major revision of the standard is expected to be released in 2017.

C++ Basic Terminology

Of course, the first step in learning the C++ programming language is to understand the basic terms. To prevent any unnecessary confusion at any point as you read this book, this section explains the most commonly used terms in the C++ program syntax. Just like the entire programming language itself, most terms in C++ are easy to remember and understand.

Bit

It is a binary digit. It is basically a variable quantity that holds exactly one of two possible values. Such values are 1 (one) or 0 (zero).

1 byte = 8 bits

1 kilobyte (KB) = 2^{10} bytes or 1024 bytes

1 megabyte (MB) = 2^{20} bytes or 1024 KB

1 gigabyte (GB) = 2^{30} bytes or 1024 MB

1 terabyte (TB) = 2^{40} bytes or 1024 GB

1 petabyte (PB) = 2^{50} bytes or 1024 TB

1 exabyte(EB) = 2^{60} bytes or 1024 PB

Compiler

Before anything else, take note that a compiler is needed to run the codes you've written with C++. Think of compilers as "translators" that convert programming language into *machine language* – the language that a computer understands. The machine language consists of only two characters (1s and 0s), which is why it is also called as *binary language*. If you're learning C++ at school, then you shouldn't worry about getting a compiler for C++ *or* an *Integrated Development Environment* for that matter.

Classes and Objects

A class is mainly used to specify an object's form as well as combine methods and data representations for the manipulation of such data into a single package. The functions and data within a class are known as *class members*.

An object is a region of storage or a contiguous region of memory with associated semantics. *First-class objects* use basic operations and can be used as you would with built-in types. *Second-class objects* require unique syntactical restrictions.

Expressions

They are a sequence of operands and operators that are used to

- Compute values from operands.

- Designate functions or objects.
- Generate side effects or actions (i.e. modifying an object's value)

They can be reduced to a value of a certain type. They also tend to be nested and are most likely a combination of simpler and smaller expressions. Primitive expressions can no longer be reduced. Some examples include identifiers and numbers.

Integrated Development Environment

An Integrated Development Environment (IDE) is essentially the software you're using to write C++ programs. It only makes sense for IDEs to come with compilers needed to run your codes. If you have no experience with C++ programming and attempting to learn it on your own, you can opt for a free C++ IDE such as *Code::Blocks*. A good choice for complete beginners is to opt for a simple C++ IDE such as *Quincy 2005* since there is very little setup required.

Lifetime

It refers to the runtime property of an object. Every object has a beginning and an end. The lifetime of objects of aggregate or class types that have been initialized by anything aside from the *trivial default constructor* starts at the end of initialization.

The lifetime of objects of class types that were not called by a *trivial destructor* ends upon the start of the destructor's execution. The lifetime of array objects, non-class objects, and class objects that have been initialized by trivial default constructors starts upon the allocation of the object's storage. Their lifetime ends when their storage are reused or deallocated.

Scope

It refers to the region of the program. In general, variables can be declared in these three places:

- Local variables, which are variables that have been declared within a function or block.
- Global variables, which are defined outside of all functions and at the top of the program.
- Formal parameters, which are variables found in the function definition.

Variables and Parameters

Variables are individual blocks in the program's memory that contains a given value. A value may be set as a constant, determined by the value of other variables using operators, or set/changed through user input. Variables are denoted by variable names or *identifiers*. In programming with C++, you can use any variable name you desire as long as all characters are valid. Remember that only alphanumeric characters and "underscores" (_) can be used in identifiers. Punctuation marks and other symbols are not allowed.

Keep in mind that variables always need to be *declared* first before they can be used. Declaring variables are different from deciding their actual values; meaning both processes are done in two different codes. These processes will be explained in the next chapter.

"Parameters" work the same way as regular variables. In fact, they are even written in the same syntax. However, parameters and variables are initialized in different ways. Parameters are specifically included in *functions* to allow arguments to be passed to a separate location from which the functions are called.

Grammar

It refers to the formal definition of the programming language. It is basically a set of rules that specify which symbol combinations are legal and which ones are not. It also specifies how such combinations are evaluated. Grammar is of utmost importance because it defines the language clearly. Modern languages, including C++, are defined using Backus-Naur Form or Backus Normal Form (BNF), which is a notation technique for context-free grammar and is used for describing the syntax of a programming language.

Parse

It refers to the analysis of an object. In C++, it usually means to break a statement, expression, or program into different components.

Expansion

It pertains to the process of replacing the function call statement with the function code by the compiler.

Statements

Every program written with C++ consists of different lines of code that performs tasks such as setting variables, calling functions, and other expressions. These lines are *statements*. Each individual statement always ends with a semicolon (;). More importantly, statements in a function are executed chronologically based on which comes first. Of course, this order can be altered using *flow control statements* such as "if statements" and "loops".

Type

It refers to the rules for

- Syntax that involves identifiers which have been declared to have it.

- Translating symbol sequences or symbols into specific numbers of bits.

You have to keep in mind that a type can be inexact or exact. The basic built-in types in C++ are *float, int, char,* and *bool.* All of these are exact, except for *float.* Exact types are sometimes referred to as *integral* since they signify discrete quantities. On the other hand, inexact types are mostly floating-point since they are usually rounded approximations.

Void, enumerations, array types, pointer types, programmer-defined types, and reference types are derived from such built-in types. Void basically refers to the absence of storage size or translation rule. This is why some people consider it to not be a proper type. Because of this, void is also referred to as syntactic type in order to differentiate it from the others.

There are certain variations to the *float* and *int* types that you have to take note of. You have to pay special attention to *double*, which is similar to *float*, except that it has two times more digits. In almost all purposes, the approximate values have to be stored as *doubles* instead of *floats.*

In addition, built-in type definitions may differ. For instance, the *int* you see on your computer may have a different definition from the *int* on an older, newer, smaller, or larger computer that runs on either a different or similar operating system. Since individual bits are usually not addressable, *bool* data types have the same size or number of bits as *char* data types.

Functions

Functions are blocks in a C++ program structured to complete a group of statements. You can call upon functions at any point whilst the program is running. Curly brackets or braces ({}) enclose the statements or "body" in each function. Aside from a function name, functions are also set with corresponding "types" which refer to the requested form of *returned value*. You can also use and set parameters at the beginning of each function. They are enclosed in parentheses "()" and separated using commas (,).

In C++, the following is the most used syntax when creating functions:

```
"type" "name" ( parameter 1, parameter 2,
parameter 3, …)
{
    "statements";
}
```

Blocks

A block is a group of statements which the compiler treats as a single statement and is enclosed by braces { }. A block of statements is also referred to as a *compound statement*. Blocks can be used anywhere where a single statement can be used. A semicolon is no longer necessary to be placed after the closing brace.

Whitespace

It refers to the characters used for the purpose of formatting. In C++, it mainly refers to tabs, spaces, and newlines. It is usually ignored by the compiler, except in certain conditions. Only one whitespace is necessary to separate tokens. When writing a program, you should not be reluctant to use as many whitespaces as you want. They can help you as well as other people read and understand the program better.

Friends

They are classes or functions declared with the keyword *friend*. Both protected and private members of a class can be accessed by non-member functions if they are declared as friends of that particular class. This can be done by including a declaration of the external function within the class and using the keyword *friend*.

Accessor

Accessors are member functions that retrieve the contents of protected data members. In order for an accessor to perform its function, it should have the same type as the returned variable, as well as not have any arguments.

Mutator

Mutators are member functions that edit the contents of protected data members. In order for a mutator to perform its function, it has to have a parameter, which is the value assigned to a data member. This parameter should have the same type as the data member. There is no need for a mutator to return a value.

Comments

When working on particularly bigger projects, most experienced programmers use "comments" that can be used as descriptions for specific sections in a C++ program. Comments are completely ignored by a compiler and can therefore ignore proper coding syntax. Comments are preceded either by a *two slashes* (//) or a *slash-asterisk* (/*). You will find comments in the examples throughout this book to help you understand them. A quick example would be the *"Hello World!"* program below. Of course, you can also use comments in your future projects for reference and debugging purposes.

Declaration

A declaration introduces a name into a program and occurs at least once. Structures, classes, user-defined types, and enumerated types can all be declared for compilation units. However, you should take note that multiple declaration requires for all declarations to be exactly the same. A declaration can also serve as a definition, except when it

- Is a function prototype or a function declaration without a function body.
- Has an *extern* storage class specifier but does not have an initializer or a function body.
- Is of a static data member in a class declaration.

- Is a *typedef* statement.
- Is a class name declaration without a definition.

Definition

Definition refers to the unique specification of a variable, class, enumerator, function, or object. Only one definition per program element is allowed for every program since definitions have to be unique. A certain program element cannot be defined but can be declared when

- The function is declared but not referenced with an expression taking its address or a function call.
- The class can be used without identifying its definition. Take note, however, that the class has to be declared.

Concatenation

It refers to the process of appending a string to the end of another string. You can concatenate string constants or string literals using the plus (+) operator. When you do this, the compiler creates a string and a run time does not occur. However, you must take note that you can only concatenate string variables during run time.

The C++ Program Structure

The program structure of C++ is very easy to understand. The compiler reads every line of code from top to bottom. This is why the first part of a C++ program usually starts with *preprocessor directives* and the declaration of variables and their values. The best way to illustrate this structure is to use the most popular example in the world of C++ -- the "Hello World!" program. Take note of the lines of code as well as the comments below:

```
#include    <iostream>    //   this   is   a
preprocessor directive

int  main()  // this  line  initiates  the
function named main, which should be found
in every C++ program


{

    std::cout  <<  "Hello  World!";  //  the
    statements found between the curly braces
    make up the main function's body

    return 0; // the return 0; statement is
    required to tell the program that the
    main  function  ran  correctly.  However,
    some compilers do not require this line
    in the main function

}
```

The topmost line ("#include <iostream>") is a preprocessor directive that defines a section of the standard C++ programming library known as the Input/Output Stream or simply *iostream*. This section handles the input and output operations in C++ programs. Remember that this is important if you wish to use "std::cout" in the main function's body.

The first line "int main ()" initializes the main function. Remember that the "int" refers to the *integer* data type and he "main" refers to the function's name. There are other data types aside from int. But you should focus on the integer data type for now. Since the "Hello World!" program does not need a parameter, it leaves the space between the parentheses succeeding the function name blank. Also, bear in mind that you should NOT place a semicolon (;) after initializing functions.

Next is the function's body, denoted by the open curly brace. This particular part ("std::cout") of the program refers to the **st**andard **c**haracter **out**put device, which is the computer's display device. Next comes the *insertion operator* (<<) from the input/output stream which means the rest of the line is to be outputted (excluding quotations). Lastly, the statement is closed with a semicolon (;).

The last line in the function's body is the *return statement* ("return = 0;"). Remember that the return expression (in this example, "o") depends on the data type specified upon initialization of the function. However, it is possible to create functions without the need for return statements using the "void" function type. For example; *void main ()*.

An alternate way to do this is to include the line "using namespace std;" under the preprocessor line so you no longer need to write "std::" each time you use it. If you opt for this method, the code would look like:

```cpp
#include <iostream>

using namespace std;

int main()

{

    cout << "Hello World!";

    return 0;

}
```

Chapter 2 – C++ Variables and Operators

What You Will Learn:

**Introduction to C++ Operators and How to Use Them

**Declaring and Determining the Value of Variables

**Creating New Lines in the Program Output

In a C++ program, variables and constants are controlled or "operated" using *Operators*. Take note that the basic operators in the C++ programming language are essentially the same as arithmetic operator. This includes the equal sign (=) for assigning expressions, the plus sign (+) for addition, the minus sign (-) for subtraction, the asterisk (*) for multiplication, the forward slash (/) for division, and the *modulus* symbol or the percentage sign (%) for obtaining the remainder from any expression.

C++ also uses other operators to fulfill additional tasks other than basic arithmetic operations. As mentioned in the previous chapter, the iostream header allowed you to use the insertion operator (<<) for processing output. There are also different operators accessible even without the #include directive. These "basic" operators can be categorized under *increment/decrement operators, comparison operators, compound assignment operators,* and *logical operators.*

Declaring Variables

Before using variables in C++ operations, you must first declare them and determine their values. Again, declaring variables and giving their values are two separate processes. The syntax for declaring variables are as follows:

```
"type" "variable";
```

Just like when initializing functions, you need to specify the data type to be used for a given variable. For example; say you want to declare "x" as an integer variable. The initialization should look like this:

```
int x;
```

After the declaration of x, you can give it a value using the assign operator (=). For example; to assign the value "99" to variable x, use the following line:

```
x = 99;
```

Make sure to declare a variable first before you assign a value to it. Alternatively, you can declare a variable and assign a value to it using a single line. This can be done using:

```
int x = 99;
```

Aside from setting these expressions as you write the program, you can also use operations and user input to determine their values as the program runs. But first, you need to learn about the other operators in C++.

Increment and Decrement Operators

The increment operator consists of two plus signs (++) while the decrement operator consists of two minus signs (--). The main purpose of increment and decrement operators is to shorten the expression of adding and subtracting 1 from any given variable. For example; if x = 2, then ++x should equal 3 while −x should equal 1.

If being used to determine the values of two or more variables, increment and decrement operators can be included as either a prefix or suffix. When used as a suffix (x++ or x--), it denotes the original value of x *before* adding or subtracting 1. When run on their own, both ++x and x++ have the same meaning. But when used in setting other variables, the difference is made obvious. Here is a simple example to illustrate the difference:

```
X = 5;
Y = ++x;
```

In this example, the value of y is determined *after* increasing the value of x. In other words, the value of y in this example is equal to 6.

```
X = 5;
Y = x++;
```

In this example, the value of y is determined *before* increasing the value of x. In other words, the value of y in this example is equal to 6.

Compound Assignment Operators

Aside from basic arithmetic operators and the standard assignment operator (=), compound assignment operators can also be used to perform an operation before a value is assigned. Compound assignment operators are basically shortened versions of normal expressions that use basic arithmetic operators.

Here are some examples of compound assignment operators:

```
x -= 1; // this is the same as the expression
x = x - 1;

x *= y; // this is the same as the expression
x = x * y;
```

```
x += 1; // this is the same as the expression
x = x + 1;

x /= y;    // this is the same as the
expression x = x / y;
```

Comparison Operators

Variables and other expressions can be compared using relational or comparison operators. These operators are used to check whether a value is greater than, less than, or equal to another. Here are the comparison operators used in C++ and their description:

== - checks if the values are equal

< - checks if the first value is less than the second

> - checks if the first value is greater than the second

<= - checks if the first value is less than *or* equal to the second

>= - checks if the first value is greater than *or* equal to the second

!= - checks if the values are NOT equal

Comparison operators are commonly used in creating condition statements. They can also be used to evaluate an expression and return a *Boolean value* ("true" or "false").

Using the comparison operators listed above; here are some example expressions and their corresponding Boolean value:

```
(8 == 1) // this line evaluates to "false"
(8 > 1)  // this line evaluates to "true"
(8 != 1) // this line evaluates to "true"
(8 <= 1) // this line evaluates to "false"
```

Also take note that the Boolean value "false" is equivalent to "0" while "true" is equivalent to other non-zero integers.

Aside from numerical values, the value of variables can also be checked when using comparison operators. Simply use a variable's identifier when creating the expression. Of course, the variable must be declared and given an identified value first before a valid comparison can be made. Here is an example scenario

```
#include <iostream>
using namespace std;

int main ()

{
    int a = 3; // the values of a and b are
set first
    int b = 4;
```

```
    cout << "Comparison a < b = " << (a < b);
    return 0;
}
```

The output for this code is as follows:

```
Comparison a < b = true
```

Take note that the insertion operator (<<) is used to insert the value of the expression "a < b" in the output statement, which is denoted in the 7th line ("cout << "Comparison a < b = "...). Don't forget that you *need an output statement* in order to see if your code works. The following code will produce no errors, but it won't produce an output either:

```
#include <iostream>

int main (
{
    int a = 3;
    int b = 4;
    (a < b);
    return 0;
}
```

In this code, it is also true that a < b. However, no output will be produced since the lines necessary for the program output are omitted.

Logical Operators

There are also other logical operators in C++ that can determine the values of Boolean data. They are the NOT (!), AND (&&), and OR (||) operators. Here are specific examples on how they are used:

```
!(6 > 2)     //    the   NOT   operator   (!)
completely    reverses    any    relational
expressions   and   produces   the   opposite
result. This expression is false because 6 >
2 is correct
```

```
(6 > 2 && 5 < 10) // the AND (&&) operator
only   produces   true   if   both   expressions
correct. This expression is true because
both 6 > 2 && 5 < 10 are correct
```

```
(6 = 2 || 5 < 10) // the OR (||) operator
produces true if one of the expressions are
correct. This expression is true because the
5 < 10 is correct although 6 = 2 is false.
```

You can also use the NOT operator in addition to the other two logical operators. For example:

```
!(6 = 2 || 5 < 10) // this expression is false

!(6 > 2 && 5 < 10) // this expression is also false

!(6 < 2 && 5 < 10) // this expression is true
```

Creating New Lines

From this point on in this book, you will be introduced to simple C++ programs that produce output with multiple lines. To create new lines when producing output, all you need to do is to use the *new line character* (\n). Alternatively, you can use the "endl;" manipulator to create new lines when using the "cout" code. The main difference is that the *internal buffer* for the output stream is "flushed" whenever you use the "endl;" manipulator with "cout". Here are examples on how to use both:

```
cout << "Sentence number one \nSentence number two";
```

The example above uses the new line character.

```
cout << "Sentence number one" << endl;
cout << "Sentence number two";
```

The example above uses "`endl;`".

Of course, the first code (using \n) is relatively simpler and easier for general output purposes. Both will produce the following output:

```
Sentence number one

Sentence number two
```

You can also use **std::endl** to create a new line. It basically inserts a newline character and flushes the stream. However, take note that it is an output-only input-output manipulator that may be called with expressions, such as *out << std::endl*. You can use it if you want an immediate output. For instance, you may need a quick output when you try to display an output from a process that takes a long time to run. You may also want to have a quick output when you log activities of multiple threads or you log activities of a program that have a tendency to crash all of a sudden.

Then again, you have to take note that this is not always the case. Sometimes, using \n may result in a more immediate output. Moreover, you may need to use *std::cout* before you use *std::system*. However, you may want to avoid using *std::endl* with *std::cout* to avoid redundancy.

\n vs. std::endl

As mentioned above, if you want to have a quick output, you should opt to use *std::endl* instead of \n. While both commands send a newline character, *std::endl* flushes the output buffer while \n does not. So basically, *std::endl* includes a *flush*, which creates uncommitted changes to underlying output sequences.

Using *std::endl* instead of \n forcefully causes a *flush* to occur. If it is alright for you not to have the buffer flushed often, you can go ahead and use \n. However, you should use *std::endl* if your program is not stable yet you still want the entire output to be displayed.

It is pretty clear that *std::endl* leads to quicker results; but when can \n prove to have a much faster output? Consider the following examples. The first program uses *std::endl* while the second program uses \n.

```
#include <string>
#include <iostream>

int main ( )
{
     for (int j = 0; j < 10; ++j)
     {
          std::string a(1, 'w');
          std::cout << a << std::endl;
     }
return 0;
}


#include <string>
#include <iostream>

int main ( )
{
```

```
    for (int j = 0; j < 10; ++j)
    {
        std::string a(1, 'w');
        std::cout << a << '\n';
    }
    return 0;
}
```

If you run both programs, your output will be:

```
w
w
w
w
w
w
w
w
w
w
```

Your output is essentially the same, so you can use either of these programs. However, if you will look at their run times, you will find out that the second program is much faster. In this case, flushing the stream immediately is not necessary. You can simply use \n to put a newline character to the stream, and then use *std::flush* afterwards if necessary.

If you use \n, the performance of your output may be reduced. Likewise, the use of unnecessary *endl* can degrade your output. Also, if you have an incomplete line of output that has to be flushed, you can use *std::flush*. If you need all the characters of your output to be flushed, you can use *std::unitbuf*.

The following example makes use of both *std::endl* and \n, but no *flush* occurs:

```
#include <iostream>
int main (void)

{
    std::cout << " First Output" << std::endl;
    std::cout << "Second Output \n";
}
```

If you run this program, your output will be:
First Output
Second Output

Chapter 3 – All About User Input

What You Will Learn:

**Utilizing the Input Stream

**Using Input to Determine or Modify Values

**How to Input and Output Strings

Up to this point, you've learned how to make a C++ program that can perform arithmetic operations, comparisons, and can produce output as well. This time, you will learn how to code one of the most important aspects of computer programs – *user input*.

As stated earlier, user input can be utilized to determine or modify the values of certain variables. C++ programs use abstractions known as *streams* to handle input and output. Since you already know about the syntax for output ("`cout`"), it's time to learn about the syntax for input ("`cin`").

The Extraction Operator

The input syntax "cin" is used with the *extraction operator* (>>) for formatted input. This combination along with the *keyboard* is the standard input for most program environments. Remember that you still need to declare a variable first before input can be made. Here is a simple example:

```
int x; // this line declares the variable
identifier x. Take note of the data type
"int" which means that only an integer value
is accepted
```

```
cin >> x; // this line extracts input from
the cin syntax and stores it to x
```

User input can also be requested for multiple variables in a single line. For example; say you want to store integer values for variables x and y. This should look like:

```
int x, y; // this line declares the two
variables
```

```
cin >> x >> y; // this line extracts user
input for variables x and y
```

Take note that the program will automatically require the user to input *two* values for the two variables. Which comes first depends on the order of the variables in the line (in this case, input for variable "x" is requested first).

However, you should take note that if you ask for an integer, you will receive an integer. For example, if you input 1.3, which is a *float*, cin will return 1 and drop .3.

Here is an example of a program that extracts user input and produces an output:

```cpp
#include <iostream>    // again, this is essential for input and output
using namespace std;

int main ()

{
    int x;
    cout << "Insert a random number \n";
    cin >> x;   // this is where user input is extracted
    cout << "You inserted: " << x;
    return 0;

}
```

Bear in mind that the value extracted from the input stream overwrites any initial value of a variable. For example, if the variable was declared as "int x = 2;" but was later followed by the statement "`cin >> x;`", the new value will then replace the original value until the program/function restarts or if an assignment statement is introduced.

Strings

Keep in mind that there are other types you can assign to variables in C++. Aside from integers, another fundamental type is the *string*. A string is basically a variable type that can store sets of characters in a specific sequence. In other words, this is how you can assign words or sentences as values for certain variables.

First of all, you need to add the preprocessor directive "`#include <string>`" before you can use strings in your program. Next, you need to declare a string before it can receive assignments. For example; if you want to declare a string for "Name" and assign a value for it, you can use the code:

```
#include <string>
using namespace std;

int main ()
```

```
{
    string name;
    name =    "Insert  your  name  here";  //
including quotations
}
```

Creating output using strings is basically the same as with integers. You only need to use "cout" and insert the string to the line. The correct syntax is as follows:

```
string name;

Name = "Your Name Here";

cout << "My name is: " << name;
```

Without any changes, the output for the above code is:

```
Your Name Here
```

To make things clearer, you should consider another example. Make sure that you do not forget the string library when you write a program.

```
#include <iostream>
#include <string>
using namespace std;

int main ( )
{
    string name;
    cout << "What is your name?";
```

```
    cin >> name;
    cout << "Hi there" << name << '\n';
    return 0;
}
```

Do you see a problem with this program? If you analyze it carefully, you will notice that cin comes to a halt the moment it sees a blank character. If you enter your name and it only consists of one word, you will still get the output that you want. For example, if you input "Wendy", the program will read "Wendy". However, if you input "Wendy Dawn", "Dawn" will not be read. So what can you do so that both words can be read? You need to use **getline**.

Inputting Strings

To allow user input values for strings, you need to use the function "getline" in addition to the standard input stream "cin". The syntax for this is "getline (cin, [string]);". Below is an example program that puts string input into application.

```
#include <iostream>
#include <string>
using namespace std;

int main ()
```

```
{
    string name;
    cout << "Greetings! What is your
name?\n";
    getline (cin, name); // this is the
extraction syntax
    cout << "Welcome " << name;
    return 0;

}
```

Take note that strings have "blank" values by default. This means nothing will be printed if no value is assigned or if there is no user input.

The function **getline** is also ideal if you want your program to read a series of words. You can use it and pass in a file-associated stream or an input stream object. Consider this example:

```
#include <iostream>
#include <string>
using namespace std;

int main ( )
{
    string str_noun;
    cout << "What is your name?";
    getline (cin, str_noun);
    cout << "Hi there" << str_noun << '\n';
    cout << "Where do you live?";
```

```
        getline (cin, str_noun);
        cout << "I live in" << str_noun << '\n';
        return 0;
}
```

As you have noticed, the string variable **str_noun** was used a few times. **Str_** was also added to the name of the string to make it easier to read. Although not required, using **str_** is recommended for large programs to avoid confusion and improve organization. Anyway, when **str_noun** was used the second time, its previous value was disregarded. The new input value replaced the old one. If you run this program, you will see that your input stays recorded until you place a return statement. You may also use **getline** to add another parameter and terminate the program. Consider this example:

```
#include <iostream>
#include <string>
using namespace std;

int main ( )
{
        string str_noun;
        cout << "What is your name?";
        getline (cin, str_noun, '#');
        cout << "Hi there" << str_noun << '\n';
        return 0;
}
```

You can input your name, press Enter, your surname with #, and press Enter. In this program, '#' is the terminating character. Until the program reads '#', everything you type in will be recorded. You still need to hit return or use \n (newline). A terminating character can be highly useful, such as for parsing. Then again, you have to be extra careful when you use terminating characters with the same string variable. Consider this sample program:

```
#include <iostream>
#include <string>
using namespace std;

int main ( )
{
    string str_noun;
    cout << "What is your name?";
    getline (cin, str_noun, '#');
    cout << "Hi there" << str_noun << '\n';
    cout << "Where do you live?";
    getline (cin, str_noun);
    cout << "I live in" << str_noun << '\n';
    return 0;
}
```

If you run this program, you will realize that is not possible to have a second input. This happens because the second **getline** processes the newline while it is still in the *input buffer*. So in order for you to be able to have a second input, you need to use **cin.ignore ( );** after your initial **std::cin**. This allows for a character to be grabbed off the **input buffer** and discarded.

How about if you want to append or join two strings? What can you do? Well, you can use the arithmetic operator plus (+). Look at the following program.

```
#include <iostream>
#include <string>
using namespace std;
```

```
int main ( )
{
    string first;
    string second;
    string third;

    cout << "What is your first name?";
    getline (cin, first);
    cout << "What is your last name?";
    getline (cin, second);
    third = " " + second;
    second = third;
    third = first + second;
    cout << "Hi there" << third << '\n';
    return 0;
}
```

You can add " " to your second string if your do not want *Your Name* to be *YourName*. If you want to swap strings, you can use **second = third;** and if you want to join both strings, you can use **third = first + second;** in your program. You can also use compound assignment operators, such as +=. Remember that string concatenation continues to occur as long as you use a C++ string. Your other string can be *static* or *char*.

Chapter 4 – Using Flow Control Statements

What You Will Learn:

**If and Else Selection Statements*

**Creating Iterating/Looping Statements*

**Other Flow Control Statements*

Remember that statements are the basic building blocks of a program written using C++. Each and every line that contains expressions such as a variable declaration, an operation, or an input extraction is a statement.

However, these statements are *linear* without some form of flow control that can establish the "sense" or "logic" behind a C++ program. This is why you should learn how to utilize flow control statements such as *selection statements* and *looping statements.*

If and Else Statements

If and else statements are the most basic form of logic in a C++ program. Basically, the main purpose of an "if" statement is to allow the execution of a specific line or "block" of multiple statements only *if* a specified condition is fulfilled.

Next is the "else" statement which allows you to specify what would occur in case the conditions aren't met. Without an "else" statement, everything inside the "if" statement will be completely ignored. Here the syntax for an "if" and "else" statement:

```
if (age >= 18)
    cout << "You are allowed to drink.";
else
    cout << "You are not yet allowed to
drink.";
```

Remember that conditions can only be set using comparison operators and logical operators (refer to Chapter 2). Take note that you can also execute multiple statements using if/else conditions by enclosing the lines in curly braces. It is also possible to use composite conditions using logical operators such as AND (&&) and OR (||).

Finally, you can use another "if" statement after an "else" statement for even more possibilities. Of course, you also need to specify conditions for every "if" statement you use.

Here is a good example that demonstrates what you can do using "if" and "else" statements in addition to user input:

```
#include <iostream>
using namespace std;

int main()

{
    int number;
    cout << "Enter a number from 1-3\n";
    cin >> number;
    if (number == 1 || number == 2)
        cout << "You have entered either 1 or
2.";
    else if (number == 3)
        cout << "You have entered 3.";
    else
    {
        cout << "Please follow the
instructions\n";
        cout << "Please Try Again.";
    }
    return 0;
}
```

There are 3 possible outcomes in the program above. The first outcome is achieved if the user entered any of the numbers 1 or 2. The second outcome is achieved if the user entered the number 3. Lastly, the third outcome is achieved if the user entered a different number other the ones specified.

Creating Choices (Yes or No)

Another way to utilize if/else statements is to create "Yes or No" choices. For this, you need to make use of the variable type "char" which can hold a character from the *8-bit character set* (you can use char16_t, char32_t, or wchar_t for larger character sets; but this is not usually necessary). Just like all other variables, a "char" variable needs to be declared before it can be used.

Of course, you want the user to make the choice, which is why you need to use the "cin" function to extract user input. Here is a simple program that asks for the user's gender:

```
#include <iostream>
using namespace std;

int main()
```

```
{
    char gender; // this is the char variable
declaration
    cout << "Male or Female? (M/F)";
    cin >> gender; // user input is stored to
gender
    if (gender == 'm' || gender == 'M')
        cout << "You have selected Male.";
    else if (gender == 'f' || gender == 'F')
        cout << "You have selected Female.";
    else
        cout << "Please follow the
instructions.";
    return 0;

}
```

Take note that you should use *single quotation marks* (')
when pinpointing "char" values. In C++, "char" values are
always called inside single quotation marks. Additionally,
remember that "char" values are case-sensitive, which is
why the example above used the OR (||) operator in the
conditions to accept both lowercase and uppercase answers.
You can see that the program above checked if the user
entered 'm', 'M', 'f', or 'F'.

Looping Statements

Lastly, using "loops" allow statements to be executed for a set number of times or until a condition is met. By incorporating other statements in loops, you can do far more than just create pointless repetitions. But first, you need to be familiar with the different types of loops.

There are 3 types of loops in C++ -- *while, do,* and *for.*

While Loop

The *"while loop"* is regarded as the simplest form of loop in the C++. Basically, it repeats the statement(s) as long as the given condition is true. Keep in mind that your code should be structured to eventually fulfill the condition; otherwise you might create an "infinite loop".

Here is an example of a while loop:

```
int x = 100;

while (x >= 0) // the condition for the loop
is set
    {
    cout << x;
    --x;     // the value of x is decreased
    }
```

In this example, the loop executes as long as the value of x is greater than or equal to 0. Take note of the decrement operator (--) in the statement "--x;". This makes sure that the value of x is continually decreased until the condition is met and the loop ends.

Do-While Loop

The next type of loop is the *"do-while loop"*. The do-while loop is essentially the same as the while loop. The main difference is that the do-while loop allows the execution of the statement(s) at least *once* before the condition is checked. Whereas in the while loop, the condition is checked *first*.

Here is an example of a do-while loop:

```
int x = 100;
int y;

do

    {

    cout << "The value is " << x << "\n";
    cout << "Enter a value to subtract.";
    cin >> y;
    x -= y;
    }
```

```
while (x > 0); // in the do-while loop, the
condition is checked last
```

In the example above, the statements are executed at least once before the value of x is checked. Whereas in a while loop, there is a possibility that the statement(s) will not be executed at all.

For Loop

The third type of loop is the *"for loop"* which has specific areas for the *initialization, condition,* and *increase.* These three sections are sequentially executed throughout the life cycle of the loop. By structure, for loops are created to run a certain number of times because increment or decrement operators are usually used in the "increase" section.

Here is the syntax for this loop to help you understand it better:

```
for (int x = 10; x > 0; x--)
```

Notice the three expressions inside the parentheses (int x = 10; x > 0; x--) are separated in semicolons. These parameters denote the three sections of the loop. You may also use multiple expressions for each section using a comma (,). Here is the syntax for this:

```cpp
for ( int x = 10, y = 0; x != y; --x, ++y )
    {
    cout << "X and Y is different\n";
    }
```

In this example, the loop is executed as long as x is not equal to y. And in order for the loop to end, the values of x and y are adjusted until the value of x equals the value of y. Based on the parameters above, the statement "x and Y is different" will run a total of 5 times before the loop is ended.

Remember that inserting expressions inside the three fields for the initialization, condition, and increase is completely optional. These fields can be left empty and the functions inside the loop will remain operational. However, semicolons (;) must always be inserted in their appropriate locations regardless if expressions are inserted or not. Here is an example:

```
for ( ; x != y ; --x)
```

Notice that the section for the initialization is left blank. A common scenario in which this occurs is when the needed values are already initialized beforehand.

Other Flow Control Statements

Aside from the loop statements, other statements such as the *break* statement, the *goto* statement, and the *continue* statement alters the flow of the program. These are called jump statements. They transfer program control within functions unconditionally.

Break Statement

The break statement serves as a forced exit from a loop. Whenever the break statement is called, the program leaves a loop; disregarding the need for completing any existing conditions. Break statements can be used to end infinite loops or to end a loop whenever necessary. To use the break statement, simply insert `break;` wherever you need to exit the loop.

Here is an example of a loop being terminated by the break statement:

```
for (int x = 5; x > 0; x--)
    {
    cout << x << ", ";
    if (x == 1)
        {
        cout << "Timer aborted.";
        break;
        }
    }
```

Continue Statement

The continue statement can be used to proceed with the next iteration of the loop without running any other statements coming after it. Usually, the continue statement is used after setting a condition; otherwise everything will be skipped throughout the life cycle of the loop. To use the continue statement, insert continue; after a set condition and *before* the statement(s) to be skipped.

Here is an example of a loop using the continue statement to skip a particular iteration:

```
for (int x = 150; x > 0; x--)
    {
    if (x == 25) continue;
    cout << x << ", ";
    }
    cout << "Find the missing number!\n";
```

Goto Statement

The goto (literally *go to*) statement is useful for accessing any section of the program. Bear in mind that goto statements can completely disrupt the flow of the program and may cause complications and undesired results, especially when used between statement blocks that share similar variables. Goto statements are generally considered as unnecessary in professional coding. However, goto statements can make simple alternatives for looping statements.

Before a goto statement can be used, you must first set a *label* which acts as a marker for a possible destination. To set a label, insert any acceptable identifier and immediately close it with a colon (:). To use a goto statement, simply insert `goto` followed by the desired label's identifier (excluding the colon) and close it with a semicolon (;).

Here is an example of a loop created using the goto statement:

```
int main ()

{
int x = 20;
loopstart: // this is a properly set label
cout << x << ", ";
x--;
if (x > 0) goto loopstart; // the program
jumps back to the label loopstart:
cout << "Countdown Complete!"\n";
}
```

Remember to always set conditions before using goto statements. In this particular example, the program is instructed to return to the `loopstart:` label as long as the value of x is greater than 0.

Exit Function

Its main purpose is to end the program before its normal termination. You can stop your program at any time by using the exit function, whose standard format is *exit (code);* wherein code is an integer. o is usually used for the value of the code, but such value may vary depending on your operating system.

Here is an example of a program using the exit function:

```
#include <stdio.h>
#include <stdlib.h>

int main ( )
{
    FILE * pFile;
    pFile = fopen ("sample message", "x");
    if (pFile == NULL)
    {
        printf ("exit message");
        exit (EXIT_FAILURE);
    }
    else
    {
    }
    return o;
}
```

If you run this program, you will get an output of:

exit message

If you notice, the program used two headers: *stdio.h and stdlib.h. Stdio.h* is the standard buffered I/O while *stdlib.h* defines variable types, macros, and functions.

Chapter 5 – Using Switch Statements

What You Will Learn:

**The Syntax for Using Switch Selection Statements

**How Switch Selection Statements Are Used

**Incorporating Switch Statements with Other Flow Control Statements

Using the switch selection statement is the last thing you need to learn as a novice in C++. The switch statement works by checking the value of *constant* expressions and running a group of statements or *cases*. Cases are then closed using break statements.

The syntax for initializing a **switch** statement is `switch (expression)` and the cases to be included will be enclosed in curly braces ({}). The *expression* is basically the identifier of the constant to be used in the switch selection statement.

The syntax for creating **cases** is `case constant:` followed by the group of statements to be executed and the break statement.

The purpose of using the switch selection statement is slightly similar to using if-else statements. The main difference is that switch selection statements are limited to constants. Moreover, you can easily create a number of different possibilities using a switch selection statement.

For example, when creating choices using if-else statements, you need to create multiple *if* or *else if* statement blocks for each condition. On the other hand, you can set as many cases as you like when using the switch selection statement. Lastly, the label `default:` acts as the final *else* statement, meaning a switch selection statement will execute default if no previous cases are fulfilled. Also remember that the default label is optional.

Here is the typical example of a switch selection statement:

```
switch (n)  // in this particular example,
the constant value of x is checked
{
    case 1:
        cout << "The value of 'N' is 1";
```

```
        break;
    case 2:
        cout << "The value of 'N' is 2";
        break;
    case 3:
        cout << "The value of 'N' is 3";
        break;
    default:
        cout << "Unable to determine the
value of 'N'";
}
```

Notice that unlike case statements, you no longer need to use the break statement for default. Without the break statement, any other statements – even those within different cases – will be executed until another flow control statement is used or until the switch ends.

Finally, remember that due to its limitations, switch selection statements are best used only for constants with integer and character values. The use of logical operators is not possible when initializing switches or declaring cases, although they can be used inside the statement block. Using switch selection statements when working with strings may also be possible by using *hash values*, but it is nowhere near as efficient as using if-else statements when it comes to strings.

Here is an example of a switch statement to help you understand it further:

```cpp
#include <iostream>

int main ( )
{
    std::cout << "Would you like to continue (yes or no)?\n";
    char response = 0;
    std::cin >> response;

    switch (response)
    {
        case 'a':
            return true;
        case 'b':
            return false;
        default:
            std::cout << "Your response is undetermined.\n";
            return false;
    }
}
```

Running this program will yield to an output of:

Would you like to continue (yes or no)?
Your response is undetermined.

When writing a program with a *switch statement*, see to it that your case constants are distinct. If you do not want to include a default statement, you may skip it.

Activity: Color Program using Flow Control Statements

Knowing the functions of flow control statements is meaningless if you don't know how to apply them in a program. To make sure you're keeping up with everything you've learned so far, you need to see these statements in action. Feel free to create any changes to these codes and try running them using your IDE.

By now you should already have a working IDE for learning C++. If you're a student, you should be able to request a copy from your instructor. If not, you can refer to Chapter 1 when looking for a standalone IDE application. Below is an example program that utilizes a switch statement integrated within a loop. Each important section is marked with comments. To fully understand what each section does and how it works, refer to the explanations on each section at the end of the chapter.

```
#include <iostream>

using namespace std;
```

```cpp
int main ()

{

    bool valid = true; // Section 1
    char color;

    cout << "Welcome.  Choose   a   primary
color!\n
    Please enter R for Red, B for Blue, and Y
for Yellow";

    while (valid) // Section 2

    {

        cin >> color;

        if (color == 'b')   // Section 3
        {

            color = 'B';

        }
        else if (color == 'r')
            {

                color = 'R';

            }
            else if (color == 'y)

                {
```

```
                    color = 'Y';

            }

    switch (color) // Section 4

    {

    case 'B':
        cout << "You chose blue!";
        valid = false;
        break;
    case 'R':
        cout << "You chose red!";
        valid = false;
        break;
    case 'Y':
        cout << "You chose yellow!";
        valid = false;
        break;
    default:
        cout << "Please input a valid
answer.";

        }

    }
```

```
return 0;

}
```

Section 1 – Initializing values in the program

The first section contains your standard initialization statements. Notice that the data types *char* and *bool* are used since they fit the functions required in this program most appropriately. Section 1 also contains the initial output code in order to prompt the user to choose between any of the three primary colors.

Section 2 – Checking for a valid answer

The second section initializes a *while* loop that executes depending on the Boolean value of *valid,* which was initialized in the previous section. Remember that the statements inside a while loop will execute when the expression is evaluated to be true. Once the user provides a valid input, this value will be changed to false – thereby ending the loop.

Section 3 – Checking for lowercase input

In this section, lowercase input is changed to uppercase. For example, when the user inputs lowercase 'y', the uppercase value 'Y' is saved instead. Keep in mind that logical operators can't be used when declaring cases in switch statements. Therefore, inserting lowercase answers – regardless if they correspond to a valid answer or not – will automatically result in a default. Finally, take note that there is the far more convenient function -- `toupper()`– which will be discussed in the last chapter of this book.

Section 4 – The switch statement

Finally, section 4 contains a switch statement that executes different cases based on the user's input. Again, remember that cases are closed with the break statement. Also make sure to include a statement to change the Boolean value of valid to false, otherwise the while loop will repeat infinitely.

Chapter 6 – More on Functions & Data Types

What You Will Learn:

**Calling Other Functions

**Working with Arrays

**Passing Arguments to Other Functions

Before you proceed with this chapter, remember that you are free to use the previous chapters as reference. The later chapters of this book will require you to fully understand the basics of C++ programming from the ground up. If there is something in any particular chapter that isn't clear to you, now would be a good time to review those chapters.

Separate functions outside of the main function can also be created in the same program. However, don't forget that only the `main ()` function is called upon automatically when running a program. All other functions are called using the identifiers associated with them when they were initialized. You can find the syntax for initializing functions in chapter 1.

A simple way to utilize separate functions is to pass arguments through them and return a resulting value. Basically, functions can extract values from the main function (or any other function that calls it) and save them on the specified parameters when the function was initialized.

Calling Functions

Here is a simple example on how to call other functions from the main function:

```cpp
#include <iostream>
using namespace std;

int distribute (int x, int y) // this is the
distribute function
{
    int z;
    z = x / y;
    return z;
}

int main () // this is the main function
{
    int a;
    int b;
```

71

```
    int c;
    cout << "How many pies are there?\n";
    cin >> a;
    cout << "How many people are there?\n";
    cin >> b;
    c = distribute (a, b); //the function is
called here
    cout << "Each person will receive " << c
<< " pie(s)
    each.";

}
```

In the main function, the user is prompted to insert the number of *pies* as well as the number of *people* to share the pies. Upon entering the appropriate numbers, the main function calls the `distribute` function to divide the number of pies with the number of people to calculate the most even distribution of pies.

A function can use the return statement to go back to where it was called. Notice how the values of a and b from the main function is sent to the distribute function where the value of c will be evaluated. Take a look at the diagram below:

```
int distribute (int x, int y)
                     ↑      ↑
c = distribute (     a,      b)
```

In the distribute function, the value of `z` is then returned using the return statement.

Finally, the return statement ends the called function and returns the program to where the function was originally called. In this particular example, the program returns to the point after the line `c = distribute (a, b);` -- where the final value of c will be printed.

Take note that his is only a simple example to illustrate what you can do with multiple functions. It is also possible to work with several functions that call upon each other in a chain. But with functions as small as the example given above, it is far more desirable to simply include the statements of the other function inside the main function.

Arrays

An array can be used to save a large amount of data while maintaining a functional structure. In arrays, data are contiguously stored and operates under the same name. In other words, arrays are basically groups of data using the same identifier. Each data contains values that can be accessed or referenced to individually.

Here is the syntax for declaring arrays:

```
type name [index];
```

Just like when declaring functions and variables, you always start by identifying the data type you wish to associate with an array. Next is the array 'name' or the identifier you wish to associate with the array. Finally, you have to specify the *number of data* that can be stored in the array. This should be an integer and must be enclosed in brackets ([]). This is also syntactically known as the *index*.

Keep in mind that the index does not represent a value; rather, it represents how many *values* can actually exist inside the array. These values are also called as *elements*. For example, if you wish to declare an array that can contain a total of 10 elements with integer values, you can use the syntax `int myarray [100];`.

In the earlier C language, there was no fixed data type to handle strings. This is why arrays containing characters were used. To declare arrays that stores character data, simply declare it using the syntax `char myarray [y];`. In this case, the value y represents the number of individual characters that can be stored in myarray.

Setting Values to Elements

When an array is first declared, all elements inside it will not contain any value. There are two ways for elements to receive values. One, a value may be given to an element upon initializing an array. Two, a value may be given to an element by individually referencing its index in a statement later on.

Here is the correct syntax for setting values for the elements of an array upon initialization:

```
int myarray [10] = { 1, 3, 5, 7, 9, 11, 13,
15, 17, 19 };
```

It is important to remember that the indices of an array always start with 0. If you create an array with 10 elements, the indices referring to each element are 0, 1, 2, 3, 4, 5, 6, 7, 8, and 9. Based on this example, the values of each element in myarray are:

```
myarray [0] = 1
myarray [1] = 3
myarray [2] = 5
```

```
myarray [3] = 7
...
```

Of course, you may also set these values using statements after declaring an array. For example, you can set the value of myarray [1] to 2 using the syntax:

```
myarray[1] = 2;
```

Accessing an element is also as simple as referencing it using its index. For example, if you wish to access the value of the *fifth* element of `myarray`, you can simply use the expression `myarray[4]`.

When initializing arrays, you can always leave the index blank (the number between the brackets). If this is used, the compiler automatically adjusts the value of the index to the number of elements entered upon initialization. For example, using the syntax `int myarray [] = {1, 2, 3, 4, 5};` automatically sets the index to [5].

Array Dimensions

A standard array using one index is considered as a 1-dimensional array. However, you can also create *multidimensional arrays* which utilize 2 or more indices. To help you understand this, visualize a 1-dimensional array as a graph with a single row:

```
[0] [1] [2] [3] [4]
```

```
myarray    1   3   5   7   9
```

In a 1-dimensional array, a single index may only contain 1 value. However, you can also create an array *within* an array to store more value in a single index. This is also referred to as a *bidimensional* array.

For example, you can declare a 5x5 bidimensional array using the syntax:

```
int myarray [5][5];
```

This array can be visualized as:

```
          [0] [1] [2] [3] [4]
```

```
myarray    [0]
```

```
          [1]
```

```
          [2]
```

```
          [3]
```

```
          [4]
```

It is also possible to use as many dimensions as you can when using arrays. However, bear in mind that each new dimension you add in an array significantly increases the amount of memory needed for it. When it comes to arrays, there is hardly any application for anything beyond 2-dimensional.

When referencing an element from a 2-dimensional array, you should include both indices from each dimension. For example; say you want to refer to the element marked in the array below:

```
          [0] [1] [2] [3] [4]

myarray       [0]

       [1]              y

       [2]        x
```

The element marked with 'x' is the element `myarray` `[2][1]` while the element marked with 'y' is the element `myarray [1][2]`.

As far as applications go, arrays are effective for creating structured data *and* for representing 2-dimensional fields such as the playing boards for *minesweeper, chess,* and *tic tac toe.*

Passing Arrays to Other Functions

In the C++ language, there is no means of passing an entire array to another function and use them for arguments. However, function parameters can accept an array's address, meaning it can access the local values from its source. This is essentially the same process and does in fact, save memory by eliminating the need to save a new set of data.

In order for this to happen, an array type can be declared in a function's parameters – but only with an undefined index. In other words, this simply means the function parameter may accept any array sent to it regardless of its index size. However, the data type of an array to be sent must match that of the function's parameter.

For example, you can initialize a function with the following syntax:

```
void arrayfunction (int array[])
```

You may then pass an array to the one initialized in the previous function. For example, you can initialize an array from a separate function using the syntax:

```cpp
int arraytopass [] = {1, 2, 3};
```

Next, you can pass these values to arrayfunction using the statement:

```cpp
arrayfunction (arraytopass);
```

Here is an example program with a function that prints the elements of an array from the main function:

```cpp
#include <iostream>
using namespace std;

void arrayfunction (int myarray[], int sequence)
{

    for (int n = 0; n < sequence; ++n)
        cout << myarray[n] << " ";
    cout << "\n";

}

int main ()
{

    int arraytopass[] = {1, 2, 3, 4, 5};
    arrayfunction (arraytopass, 5);
```

}

In this particular example, the array `arraytopass[]` from the main function was passed to `arrayfunction` as well as a matching integer value for `sequence`. To explain the relevance of these expressions, take a look at `arrayfunction`. Here is a closer look on the following statements:

```
arrayfunction (int myarray[], int sequence)
```

When initializing `arrayfunction`, the parameters for **myarray[]** and **sequence** were used. The `sequence` value is important since the function uses a loop that runs depending on the number of elements. Since the number of elements will be decided from a separate function (in this example, the main function), the value for the variable `sequence` was left blank upon initializing `arrayfunction`. Thus, it is open to receiving any integer value from another function.

```
int arraytopass[] = {1, 2, 3, 4, 5};
arrayfunction (arraytopass, 5);
```

In the main function, the array `arraytopass[]` was initialized along with its elements. Notice the statement immediately after the initialization statement for the array. This is where `arrayfunction` was called. This is also where the expressions from the main function that matches the parameters in `arrayfunction` were passed. Take a look at the diagram below:

```
void    arrayfunction   (int   myarray[],   int
sequence)
```

```
    arrayfunction (arraytopass,       5);
```

Finally, the value of `sequence` corresponds to the number of elements in `arraytopass[]`. This is because the function utilizes a basic decaying loop that outputs each element in the array in a sequential manner. In this particular example, you should set the value of `sequence` to 5 since there is a total of 5 elements in the array.

Chapter 7 – All About Randomization

What You Will Learn:

**Generating Random Numbers

**Setting the Maximum and Minimum Random Values

**Understanding and Setting Seeds

**Creating a Simple Dice Game

With C++, programmers can write programs that can perform virtually any task. It is just a matter of identifying exactly what it needs to do and selecting the right codes to use. Once these codes are structured correctly, the program will *always* run its course as expected. However, *randomization* is sometimes important to increase the number of possible outcomes in a program.

Generating Random Numbers

In a lot of examples from the previous chapters, most initialized variables contain values set either by you -- the coder -- or by the user through input. This time, you will learn how to create a function that generates random integer values. This decreases the predictability of your program and therefore makes it a little less boring.

First of all, you need to use the preprocessor directive `#include <cstdlib>` for creating a random number generator. This stands for the *C Standard Library* which contains the function `rand()`. Basically, you can call upon this function at any time and extract a random value just like how you would from a variable.

Using the output expression, you can use the following statement to display a random number in your program:

```
cout << rand();
```

However, bear in mind that simply using the simple statement above will generate a number from a *huge range* of values. In most programming cases, you want to limit the range of random values that the `rand()` function can generate. For example, if you want to write a code that simulates a die, you want to set the minimum value to 1 and the maximum value to 6. Or if you're trying to simulate a game of bingo, you want to generate a random number from the range of 1-75.

Setting the Maximum Random Number

To set a specific range for a randomly generated number, you can use the *modulus* operator (%) with the `rand()` function. Remember that the modulus operator works by dividing any number while extracting the remainder. When used with the `rand()` function, a random number is continually divided with the given value until a remainder can be extracted. For example, take a look at this expression:

```
rand()%75
```

Take note that any randomly generated number will either be perfectly divisible by 75 or leave a remainder. In the example above, the remainders 0-74 may be returned by the function. When the random number *30,000* is generated and is repeatedly divided by *75,* you will end up with the remainder of *5.333333* which is then rounded off to 5.

Remember that the `rand()` function uses the set of *whole numbers,* meaning the number 0 is also included. In most cases, you only want to include whole *counting* numbers starting from 1. If this is the case, you only need to add *1* to the resulting number from the `rand()` function. To do this, simply use the following syntax:

```
1+rand()
```

Of course, you can do this while setting a specific range. For example, here is an expression that extracts a random number from 1-75:

```
1+(rand()%75)
```

Here is an example program that randomly generates a number from the range 1-75:

```
#include <iostream>
#include <cstdlib>
using namespace std;

int main()
{

    cout << 1+(rand()%75);

}
```

Setting the Minimum Random Number

You may also specify the minimum random number using a simple set of arithmetic operations. Of course, you can simply set the minimum number by adding its value to the rand() function as shown above. However, take note that this will also affect the maximum number; making it tricky to come up with the correct expression for the result you desire.

So in order to set the minimum random number independently, you can use the following expression:

rand() % ('*max*' – '*min*' + 1) +'*min*';

Using this formula, you can easily set the specific minimum and maximum random number. Simply replace 'max' with the maximum number and 'min' with the minimum number. For example; say you want to generate a random number from 10-20. The correct syntax should look like:

```
rand()%(20 - 10 + 1)+ 10;
```

When using these expressions and statements in your codes, you may notice that the generated number will remain the same if you run the program twice or more in a row. This is because even though you've instructed the program to generate a random number, it still follows a set algorithm or *seed* that determines randomness.

Understanding Randomness

Keep in mind that nothing in computers is actually random. Even though a program may generate a set of random numbers to humans, the computer itself is still following an algorithm that ultimately tells it exactly how to behave. For example, the rand() function is still basically just a function with a set of instructions that returns pseudorandom results.

For example, go ahead and use the following codes to write a program and try running it:

```
#include <iostream>
#include <cstdlib>
using namespace std;

int main()

{

    for (int x = 0; x < 10; x++)
        {
            cout << rand()%(20 - 10 + 1)+ 10
<< ", ";
        }

}
```

Notice that this is a code for generating *10* random numbers from 10 to 20. For example; say running the program once will give you the following output:

```
18, 19, 19, 11, 17, 15, 15, 20, 11, 10,
```

If you are running your program as it is, then you will probably get a very similar sequence of random numbers if you are to run the program for the second time around. Of course, this is an undesirable behavior if you intend to write a program that generates randomly without being predictable.

This occurs because the program did not set a different *seed* for the random number generator. But first, you should understand what seeds are and how they are set.

Setting New Seeds

By setting a different seed, a different set of random numbers will be generated. In order to set seeds, you need to use the `srand()` function. The `srand()` function is called using the following syntax:

```
srand(expression);
```

Take note that the expression in this statement is essentially the seed you are using for the `rand()` function. For example; say you want to set the seed to 30. Your program should now look like this:

```
#include <iostream>
#include <cstdlib>
using namespace std;

int main()

{

    srand(30);

    for (int x = 0; x < 10; x++)
        {
            cout << rand()%(20 - 10 + 1)+ 10
<< ", ";
        }

}
```

Now, if you are to change the value in srand(), the program should generate a different set of random numbers. However, notice that the same set of random numbers is generated if you use the same seed each time. Essentially, you would want the program to set a different seed every single time it runs. And in order for this to happen, you need to access a value from your computer that constantly changes – your computer *time*.

To use the necessary functions for accessing your computer time, you need to use the preprocessor directive `#include <ctime>`. With this, you can call the function `time()` which basically returns the current calendar time. The returned value is usually the representation of the total number of seconds from the initiation of *UNIX Time (00:00 of January 1, 1970 UTC)*.

Basically, all you need to do is to use the returned value of `time()` to set the seed using `srand()`. This means the seed for your `srand()` function changes every second; giving you a brand new set of random numbers each time. Here is the correct syntax for setting `time()` as the expression for `srand()`:

```
srand(time(0));
```

You may also use the expression NULL in `time()` since it is also the equivalent of 0. If this is the case, the syntax would be `srand(time(NULL));`. Remember that the parameter for the `time()` function is a pointer to `time_t` type data. Most of the time, this is best left at the value 0 or NULL.

Now, go ahead and apply this statement in your previous program. Your program should now look like this:

```
#include <iostream>
#include <cstdlib>
#include <ctime> // don't forget to include
this directive
using namespace std;

int main()

{

    srand(time(0));        //        alternatively,
srand(time(NULL));

    for (int x = 0; x < 10; x++)
        {
            cout << rand()%(20 - 10 + 1)+ 10
<< ", ";
        }

}
```

You should now have a program that generates a completely random set of numbers every time it is run.

Writing a Simple Dice Game

To conclude everything you've learned up to this point, here is a sample program that simulates rolling two dice. The object of the program is to roll a 12 (both die hitting 6) to win. This is a good chance for you to practice what you've learned as the program uses three data types, a while loop, an if-else statement, and a random generator.

Before you view the written program, why not review everything you've learned and try writing it yourself? Try to write a program that does the following:

- ✓ *Prompt the user to press a particular button to roll the dice*
- ✓ *Should accept both lowercase and uppercase input*
- ✓ *Generates 2 random numbers from 1-6 to simulate two dice being rolled*
- ✓ *Gets the total of the dice*
- ✓ *Will loop the program until a total of 12 is hit*

Here is the program that does everything specified above:

```cpp
#include <iostream>
#include <cstdlib>
#include <ctime>
using namespace std;

int main()
{
```

```
srand(time(NULL));
int die1;
int die2;
int dice;
char roll;
bool round = true;

cout << "Welcome!\n";

while (round)
{
    cout << "Press 'R' to roll the dice!";
    cin >> roll;
    if (roll == 'r' || roll == 'R')
    {
        die1 = 1+(rand()%6);
        cout << "The first die rolls " << die1;
        putchar('.');

        die2 = 1+(rand()%6);
        cout << "\nThe second die rolls " << die2;
        putchar('.');
```

```
dice = die1 + die2;
cout << "\nThe total is " <<
dice;

if (dice == 12)
{
     cout << "\nRolled a 12. You
Win!";
     round = false;
}
else
{
     cout << "\nRoll a 12 to
win!\n";
}
}
}

return 0;
}
```

If you have written your own version of the program, try comparing it with this one. You may also alter any part of the program and create your own rules. Also notice that the `putchar()` function was also used twice in this program. This function's main purpose is to output a single character, as its return value is basically just the character expression.

Chapter 8 – More with C++

What You Will Learn:

**Introduction to Pointers and How to Create Them

**Passing by Reference

The C++ programming language may be considered as a novice language for some. In fact, you can probably learn and remember everything you've learned throughout this book in a day. But even so, no one can deny the fact that C++ is a very versatile and reliable language. It is still able to meet the modern demands for general purpose development.

If you are relatively new to programming, learning C++ first is an excellent first step for you to understand and appreciate the basic structure of programming. In the past few years, the programming world has shifted most of its focus to newer languages such as *C#* and *Java*. This means you will probably step into learning those modern languages in the future. But don't you worry about moving on to those languages just yet; there is still much to learn and more to do with C++.

Introduction to Pointers

Throughout this book, you learned how to declare and set different types of variables. At the moment a variable is declared, the program instructs the compiler to *reserve* an actual location in the computer's memory for that variable. For example, if you declared a variable using the syntax `int myvar;`, the program tells the compiler to interpret its value as an *integer*-type data and assigns a particular *location* in the memory for `myvar`. And that particular location is the *memory address* of the variable.

The Address-of Operator

Using the *address-of* operator (&) or the *ampersand* symbol is a very simple way to pinpoint the memory address of any given variable. The memory address will then be represented by a *hexadecimal* value upon being returned by the address-of operator.

For example; say you want to extract and print the memory address of the variable myvar and NOT its value. The syntax you can use for this purpose is:

```
cout << &myvar;
```

Keep in mind that a specific memory address of a variable cannot be identified before the program is run. This is because the particular memory location for a variable will only be assigned once the variable is declared.

Understanding Pointers

If variables can contain values of a specific type (int, char, etc.), pointers can contain *memory addresses*. In simple terms, pointers *point* to the address of a variable.

Just like variables, pointers need to be declared before they can be used. Declaring pointers also require you to specify what data type is stored in a particular address. Lastly, pointer identifiers are declared using the *asterisk* (*) symbol.

Here is the syntax for declaring a pointer in C++:

```
type *mypointer;
```

Take note that you need to declare a pointer first before you can assign an address to it. For example, you can assign `mypointer` the memory address of `myvar` using the following syntax:

```
mypointer = &myvar;
```

To help you understand pointers better, take a look at the following piece of code:

```
int myvar = 1; // myvar is initialized
int *mypointer; //mypointer is initialized
mypointer = &myvar; //the address of myvar
is assigned to mypointer
```

Suppose the memory address of `&myvar` is `0x123abc`. This value is then contained by `mypointer` while `myvar` now contains the value 1. And now that `mypointer` is containing the memory address of `myvar`, the following statements should produce the exact same output:

```
cout << &myvar;
cout << mypointer;
```

Pointers may also access the value of the variable saved in a particular address. This works by again using the asterisk symbol (*) when calling a pointer that is already declared previously. Remember that the asterisk symbol is called a *dereference operator* and not a multiplication operator if it is used with pointers. Additionally, a value can only be retrieved if a memory address is already assigned to a pointer.

For example, you can print the value of myvar by referencing it through mypointer using the statement cout << *mypointer;.

In other words, the following statements should be true:

myvar == *mypointer // both refers to the value of myvar

&myvar == mypointer // both refers to the memory address

To make sure you understand how pointers work, take a look at the following program:

```cpp
#include <iostream>
using namespace std;

int main()
{
    int myvar = 1;
    int *mypointer;
    mypointer = &myvar;
```

```
if (myvar == *mypointer)

{

    cout << "The values are correct.\n";

}

if (&myvar == mypointer)

{

    cout << "The values are correct.";

}

return 0;

}
```

In this particular example, the final output should print "*The values are correct*" twice because `myvar` and `mypointer` were set accordingly.

Using Pointers: Passing by Reference

Now that you know that pointers basically contain the memory address of a variable, you may ask; "*Why would I want a variable's memory address?*"

Memory addresses or the pointers that contain them are actually useful for passing arguments without needing to create a *copy* of a value in the receiving function. For example, if you want to pass the value of myvar to the function myfunction, you can simply pass the memory address of myvar to give myfunction direct access to the original variable. This may allow the value of myvar to be modified from within myfunction. But more importantly, the program will be more memory-efficient since it only has to work with one variable. This method of passing arguments is also called as *passing by reference.*

Here is an example program that demonstrates this:

```cpp
#include <iostream>
using namespace std;

void myfunction(int *mypointer)
{

    *mypointer = 20; //the value of myvar is
modified here

}

int main()
{

    int myvar = 0;
    myfunction    (&myvar);    //    The    memory
address is passed
```

```
    cout << "The updated value is now " <<
myvar;

    return 0;

}
```

In this particular example, notice that the address of `myvar` is passed on to `myfunction` where the original value is changed to 20. Keep in mind that in this example, both `mypointer` and `&myvar` referred to the memory address of `myvar`. Consequently, changing the value of `mypointer` changed the value stored in `myvar` since they basically worked with the same memory address.

Other Useful Functions

The standard C and C++ libraries contain many simple but useful functions. Some of these functions may already be mentioned in the previous chapters such as the `rand()` function, the `time()` and the `putchar()` function. Of course, you are always free to write your own function for various purposes.

Now that you're reaching the last chapter of this book, here is a short list of useful functions you can use to help you achieve exactly what you want from your program.

Quick Pause Function

You can create a quick and simple function that makes your computer pause for a few seconds. Remember that this is only an experimental function and that other programmers may create a unique pause function for the exact effect they desire. When called upon, this function will temporarily stop the program for around 5-10 seconds.

Here is the syntax for this function:

```
void pause()
{
    int timer = 1000000000;
    for (int x = 0; x < timer; x++)
        ;

}
```

To use this function, simply call upon it at the point where you want the program to pause momentarily. It is a useful function to use if you don't want the program to output multiple messages in quick succession.

The toupper() & tolower() Functions

In programs where the user is requested to input a character, there are instances when the lowercase letters must be translated to uppercase in order to have the desired effect. This is shown in the *Color Program* in *Chapter 5 – Using Switch Statements*.

In that particular example, the program used a chain of if-else statements that translated specific inputs to uppercase in order to accommodate the switch cases. However, you can easily translate any character input to uppercase or lowercase using the `toupper()` and `tolower()` functions. Here is a simple example on how these functions are used:

```
char first = 'x';
char second = 'Y';
first = toupper(first);
second = tolower(second);

cout << "This is changed to uppercase: " << first << endl;
```

```
cout << "This is changed to lowercase: " <<
second << endl;
```

The output for this example should look like:

```
This is changed to uppercase: X
This is changed to lowercase: y
```

In case you want to automatically change the user's input to uppercase or lowercase, you can simply use the following statements:

```
char letter;
```

```
cin >> letter;
letter    =    toupper(letter);    //    or
tolower(letter); depending  on  your  desired
effect
```

In this example, the character value of letter is immediately updated to uppercase or lowercase by applying the toupper() or tolower() function on itself.

The sizeof() Function

Basically, the sizeof() function returns the value of the size of a variable in *bytes*. In the C++ language, each data type requires a specific amount of memory in bytes. For example; in most computers, the integer data type takes up 4 bytes of memory while the character data type takes up 1 byte of memory.

On the other hand, the size of an array is dependent on the data type and the number of its elements. For example, an array containing integers with 5 elements will amount to *20* bytes (5 x 4 bytes per integer). Additionally, initializing variables using the type `double` will require twice the size of regular integers. For example, using the statement `double myvar;` will amount to *8* bytes or `double myarray[5];` will amount to *40* bytes.

Last Note

Finally, remember that any course or book that will teach you about the world of C++ will always only be guidelines. The main purpose of those materials – including this one – is to equip you with the proper tools to start your life in software development. They will not show you the exact path to take.

For many professionals, programming is a job that may eventually get tedious and exhausting. But for some people, it is the passion of a lifetime. This goes to all hardworking professionals, students, hobbyists, and other curious individuals who are now treading the exciting world of C++!

Chapter 9 – General Tips on How to Write a Program

What You Will Learn:

**General guidelines on how to create a program

**The basic steps of writing a program

**Dos and don'ts in C++

**The inline function

**Advantages and disadvantages of using inline

**When to use the inline function

Creating a program is not really that difficult. Once you understand the syntax, it will be easy for you to do the rest. You can create a flowchart to help you understand the flow of your program more easily. Sometimes, it is more effective to see something in graphic form than to describe it with words alone. Using a flowchart will allow you to explain your process more clearly and more efficiently with the use of text and symbols.

Nevertheless, when it comes to writing a program, it all boils down to six fundamental steps:

Step 1. You must write the header files and the source codes first.

Step 2. You must pre-process your source codes based on preprocessor directives, which start with a hash sign (#). Some examples are *#define* and *#include*. These codes indicate that there are symbols that may be replaced, files that may be included, and other manipulations that may occur before the compilation process starts.

Step 3. You must compile your pre-processed source codes into object codes.

Step 4. You have to link these compiled object codes with the other library codes and object codes that you have in order to produce an executable code.

Step 5. You must load this executable code into your computer's memory.

Step 6. Finally, you should run your executable code using your input in order to produce your expected output.

Of course, you need to download an Integrated Development Environment (IDE), such as Netbeans, Eclipse, and CodeBlocks. An IDE usually includes a text editor, a debugger, and a compiler. It can make programming easier and simpler. Nonetheless, you may also use a plain text editor like VIM or Notepad++.

You may also use any text editor to run programs from a command line. You may want to opt for an editor that supports line numbers and syntax highlighting. The most recommended environments for development are Unix-like operating systems, such as Linux, BSD, and OS X.

Although not necessary, you may want to use indentions and comments on your programs. Indenting your codes will make your program more organized as well as help you avoid confusion. Diving a large program into smaller section will also improve its readability.

Inserting comments will also help you avoid confusion since you will be able to see clearly what the variables and functions in your program are for. Likewise, people who are not that adept at programming will learn more about the codes that you use.

When writing comments, make sure that you capitalize global variable names. Just like writing an article or a book, you have to use uppercase and lowercase letters accordingly.

Also, see to it that you do not use deprecated functions and obfuscated styles in your program. As much as possible, you should only use simple data structures and algorithms. Too many complex codes will only generate confusion for you and your readers. You may also want to use extremely low and extremely high numbers to test the boundary conditions of your program.

Dos and Don'ts in C++

- Do minimize code in your headers.

- Do not include unnecessary headers. If the file does not use symbols from a header, you should remove the header.

- Do forward declare classes rather than include headers.

A forward declaration is ideal for almost all cases, with the exceptions of a few. For example, if it will not make any sense to use type as a member by value, you should not convert it to a pointer just so you can forward declare it. Also, you should not forward declare any symbols from the namespace v8.

- Do move inner classes into implementations.

You can forward a declare class in a class.

- Do move details of static implementation to the implementation as much as possible.

You must try to move the class in a header file into an anonymous namespace inside the implementation file. This way, the people who do not use your interface will not see it. Likewise, you can do this to improve the helper function. Take note that if there are several classes in your .cc file, they can define file-scope helpers more clearly inside an anonymous namespace.

- Do not inline code in headers.

You should not ask for the background to be inlined unless it really has to be inlined. Keep in mind that the definitions inside a class declaration tend to be inlined implicitly.

- Do not inline complex methods.

Keep in mind that an inline request is simply a suggestion. Hence, most of the operations on the integral data types are not going to be inlined. Nevertheless, each file that needs to be inlined emit a function version .o. So, if you request for an inline, you will only be adding crud to the .o files.

- Do not inline virtual methods.

In most cases, inline virtual methods cannot be inlined. The compiler has to perform a runtime dispatch using a virtual method when the compiler cannot determine the complete type of the object.

- Do refrain from inlining destructors and constructors.

Destructors and constructors are generally much more complex that you have ever imagined. This is especially true if the class has non-plain old data (POD) members. A lot of Standard Template Library (STL) classes have inlined destructors and constructors that may be copied to your function body. Since their bodies seem empty, they usually appear as trivial functions that may be inlined safely. However, you must practice self-control and not allow yourself to inline them. You should define them inside the implementation file. Remember that they seem harmless now, but in the future, they can make your destructors more complicated if you give in to the temptation of inlining them.

- Do exert extra caution in using accessors.

Keep in mind that not every accessor is lightweight.

The Inline Function

Inline functions are enhancement features that lengthen the execution time of the program. To inline a function, you simply have to use the keyword *inline* before its definition. Consider the following example:

```
class w
{
    public:
        inline int addition (int w, int d)
        {
            return (w + d);
        };
}

class w
{
    public:
        int addition (int w, int d);
};

inline int w :: addition (int w, int d)
{
    return (w + d);
}
```

When you encounter an instruction for a normal function call, your program stores the instruction's memory address immediately. It then proceeds to perform a lot of procedures, which results in too much runtime overhead. If you do not want to encounter any of this, you should use the inline function. When you use it, the process of expansion occurs and the entire code is compiled. With inline functions, there is no more need for the compiler to jump back and forth to execute its function.

Advantages and Disadvantages of Using Inline

Advantages:

- It produces quick results by avoiding overhead.
- It saves overhead of return calls from functions.
- It improves the locality of references by using instruction caches.
- It allows a function definition to be placed in a header file.

Disadvantages:

- It increases executable sizes because of code expansion.
- It may require code recompilation.
- It can make the header filer larger with unnecessary information.
- It may cause thrashing in the memory.

When Should You Use the Inline Function?

You can inline functions when performance is necessary. You can also use it over macros. Moreover, you can use inline keywords outside the class to hide details of implementation.

Chapter 10 – Character Sequences

What You Will Learn:

**Storing a character sequence in a string and an array*

**Using string literals or words placed in double quotes*

**Converting char array to string*

A character sequence is basically a readable sequence of characters values. You have learned from the previous chapters about strings and arrays. In this chapter, character sequences using strings and arrays will be discussed.

The C++ Standard Library implements a dominant string class, which can be used in manipulating strings of characters. Since strings are a character sequence, you may also use plain arrays of character elements to represent strings.

Consider this example:

char string [20];

It means that the array *string* can be used to store a maximum of twenty *char* elements. Hence, you can store a character sequence of twenty characters or less. At the end of your sequence, do not forget to use a special character to signify its termination. This special character is the null character, which you can write as \0.

Here is an example of a character sequence with a maximum of

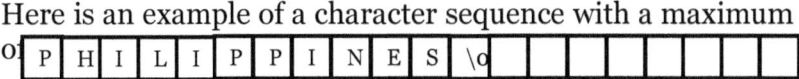

Since the word 'PHILIPPINES' has less than twenty characters, you can store it in *string*. However, you should avoid doing this because you are wasting memory. In this case, you have just wasted eight elements. Remember that a waste of elements is a waste of memory.

How about if you want to store a character sequence in an array? For example, if you want to store "WENDY" in the array *string*, you can write:

char string [ ] = { 'W', 'E', 'N', 'D', 'Y', '\o'};

This declares a six-element array of the type char. When you count the elements, do not forget to include the null character.

String Literals

These are the words you put inside double quotes. Basically, they are another way for initializing arrays of char elements with values. Using a string literal allows the null character to be automatically appended at the end. So instead of using the above codes, you can use the following to arrive at the same output:

char string [ ] = "WENDY";

To help you understand character sequence initialization further, take a look at this sample program:

```
#include <iostream>
using namespace std;
```

```
int main ( )
{
    char question [ ] = "What city do you live in?";
    char response [ ] = "I live in";
    char place [20];

    cout << question;
    cin >> place;
    cout << response << place << ".";

    return 0;
}
```

Because you declared **char place [20]**, your input can only be up to twenty characters. In this program, the first of the three arrays is asking a question while the next one is used for the answer. The third and last array is for storing the answer to the question.

Take note that you can only initialize an array of character during its declaration. If you wish to assign values to them, you may do so later on. String literals have the same restrictions as regular arrays, so values cannot be assigned to them.

If you write

```
sampleword = "Original";
sampleword [ ] = "Original";
```

or

```
sampleword = { 'O', 'r', 'i', 'g', 'i', 'n', 'a', 'l', '\0'}'
```

You will not get your desired output because they are not valid.

You cannot assign values to arrays, but you can assign individual values to the elements. For example, you can write:

```
sampleword [0] = 'O';
sampleword [1] = 'r';
sampleword [2] = 'i';
sampleword [3] = 'g';
sampleword [4] = 'i';
sampleword [5] = 'n';
sampleword [6] = 'a';
sampleword [7] = 'l';
sampleword [8] = '\0';
```

Conversion

You can convert arrays of characters to strings. Consider this sample program:

```
#include <iostream>
#include <string>
using namespace std;

int main ( )
{
       string sample_string;
       char sample_array [15] = "GOOD MORNING";

       sample_string = sample_array;
       cout << sample_string << '\n';

       return 0;
}
```

Running this program will give you the output:

GOOD MORNING

Chapter 11 – Classes

What You Will Learn:

**Declaring objects with the use of classes

**Using special functions known as constructors

**Overloading constructors

**Uniform initialization

**Classes with union and struct

**Overloading operators

Classes are expanded concepts of data structures. They contain data members, as well as functions as members.

Objects are instantiations of classes. When speaking of variables, the class is the type while the object is the variable.

In general, classes are defined using *struct* or *class*. Its general syntax is:

```
class name_of_class
{
    first_access_specifier:
        member1;
    second_access_specifier:
        member2;
```

```
    . . .
}
    name_of_object;
```

In this program, *name_of_class* is a valid identifier for class while *name_of_object* is an option for the object of the class. You can include *members* in the body of your declaration. This can be function, data, or *access specifiers*.

The format of class is the same as that of a data structure, except that it can include functions as well as have access specifiers, such as *protected*, *public*, and *private*. Such specifiers change the access rights of the members after them.

The *protected* members can be accessed from *friends* or other members of the same class, as well as from members of derived classes.

The *public* members can be accessed from any place wherein the object can be seen.

The *private* members can only be accessed from *friends* or within the other members of the same class.

All the members of a class that have been declared with the keyword *class* can be accessed privately by default. Thus, a member that has been declared prior to an access specifier automatically has a private access. Take a look at this example:

```
class rectangle
{
    int height, width;
    public:
    void values (int, int);
    int area (void);
}
```

rect;

In this program, class *rectangle* and object *rect* are declared. The class has four members, with two of them having private access and the other two having public access. The members *height* and *width* are the ones with private access, while the functions *area* and *values* have public access.

If you will take a look at the program carefully, you will notice that the class name is *rectangle* while the object of the type *rectangle* is *rect*. This is essentially the same as writing *int a*; wherein the type name is *int* and the variable name is *a*.

After you declare *rect* and *rectangle*, any public member of *rect* may be accessed as if it was a normal variable or normal function. All you have to do is place a dot between the *member name* and the *object name*. For instance, if you want to input 4 and 5 as the height and width of the rectangle, you can write it as:

```
rect.values (4, 5);
area = rect.area ( );
```

Height and width cannot be accessed externally because they only have private access. Therefore, they may only be called from within the other members of the same class.

Take a look at this full program for the *class rectangle*:

```
#include <iostream>
using namespace std;

class rectangle
{
```

```
        int height, width;
        public:
        void values (int, int);
        int area ( )
        {
              return height * width;
        }
};
void rectangle :: values (int a, int b)
{
        height = a;
        width = b;
}

int main ( )
{
        rectangle rect;
        rect.values (4, 5);
        cout << "The area of the rectangle is " << rect.area ( );
        return 0;
}
```

If you run this program, you will get an output of:

The area of the rectangle is 20

As you can see from the program, the *scope operator* is used. It consists of two colons (::) and is used in the function definition *values*. Its purpose in this program is to define a class member outside of the class.

Also, you should see from this program that the definition of *area* was directly included within the definition of *rectangle*. On the other hand, *values* was simply declared within the class, yet its definition stays outside of it. Since it is outside, *scope* is necessary for specifying that the defined function is a member of *rectangle*. If you do not use *scope*, the program will consider the function to be a non-member.

Scope also specifies which class a declared member belongs to. It grants the exact same properties as if the function definition is included directly within the class definition. In the program, the function *values* has access to variable *height* and variable *width*, which are both private members of the class *rectangle* and therefore can only be accessed from the other members of the same class.

Defining a function within the class definition and defining it outside of its class are essentially the same, except that the function is immediately regarded as an *inline member* by the compiler when you define it within the class definition. However, when you define it outside the class, it is considered as a not-inline or normal member. You will notice that there are no behavioral differences, but there are likely compiler optimization differences.

The members *height* and *width* have private access, so if you declare them as private, any access from outside of the class will no longer be allowed. It is actually pretty obvious since you have defined a member, which is *values*, to set the values for the members within the object. Hence, there is no more need for the other parts of your program to have direct access.

A class is a type that you can use to declare several objects at once. For instance, you can declare the object *rectx* aside from the object *rect*. Consider the following program:

```
#include <iostream>
using namespace std;
```

```cpp
class rectangle
{
    int height, width;
    public:
    void values (int, int);
    int area ( )
    {
        return height * width;
    }
}

void rectangle :: values (int a, int b)
{
    height = a;
    width = b;
}

int main ( )
{
    rectangle rect, rectx;
    rect.values (4, 5);
    rectx.values (6, 7);
    cout << "The area of the rectangle is " << rect.area ( )
<< endl;
    cout << "The other area is " << rectx.area ( ) << endl;

    return 0;
}
```

Running this program will give you an output display of:

The area of the rectangle is 20
The other area is 42

In the above program, the class *rectangle* has two objects, which are *rect* and *rectx*. Each of these objects has its own member functions and member variables. Also, if you noticed, calling *rect.area ( )* does not yield the same output as calling *rectx.area ( )* because each one of the objects of the class has its own variables.

Constructors

Using the above sample program, what do you think will happen if you call *area* before you call *values*? Well, if you do that, you will get an undetermined output because the members *height* and *width* have not been assigned their values yet. To prevent that from happening, you can use special functions in your class. These special functions are known as *constructors*, and they are called automatically whenever there is a new object within the class. Using them allows the class to allocate storage or initialize member variables.

You can declare constructors just as you would with regular member functions. However, you have to make sure that the name matches your class name. You should also not use any return type, including *void*. To help you understand things more clearly, consider the following sample program. It is the same as the above program with the addition of a constructor.

```
#include <iostream>
using namespace std;

class rectangle
{
        int height, width;
```

```
        public:
        rectangle (int, int);
        int area ( )
        {
             return (height * width);
        }
};

rectangle :: rectangle (int w, int d)
{
     height = w;
     width = d;
}

int main ( )
{
     rectangle rect (4, 5);
     rectangle rectx (6, 7);
     cout << "The area of the rectangle is " << rect.area ( )
<< endl;
     cout << "The other area is " << rectx.area ( ) << endl;

     return 0;
}
```

If you run this program, you will have an output of:

The area of the rectangle is 20
The other area is 42

You see, the output of this program is literally the same as the output of the previous program. However, the class *rectangle* no longer uses *values*. Instead, it uses a constructor to perform the action that *values* performed in the previous program. Just like *values*, the constructor initialized the values of height and width with the arguments that have been passed to it.

Then again, you cannot call constructors explicitly just as you would with regular member functions. You can only execute them once, and that is when a new class object is created. Also, you should take note that constructors do not return values. They only initialize objects.

Overloading Constructors

Just like any other functions, constructions may also be overloaded with various versions that take various parameters. Take a look at the following program:

```
#include <iostream>
using namespace std;

class quadrilateral
{
    int height, width;
    public:
    quadrilateral ( );
    quadrilateral (int, int);
    int area (void)
    {
        return (height * width);
    }
};

quadrilateral :: quadrilateral ( )
{
    height = 4;
    width = 5;
```

```
}

quadrilateral :: quadrilateral (int w, int d)
{
    height = w;
    width = d;
}

int main ( )
{
    quadrilateral quad (6, 7);
    quadrilateral quadx;
    cout << "The area of the quadrilateral is " << quad.area
( ) << endl;
    cout << "The other area is " << quadx.area ( ) << endl;

    return 0;
}
```

If you run this program, you will have an output of:

The area of the quadrilateral is 42
The other area is 20

As you can see, two objects of the class *quadrilateral* have been constructed and these are *quad* and *quadx*. *Quad* is constructed using two arguments.

In this program, a special type of constructor is also used. This is the *default constructor*. It does not take any parameters and it is called whenever an object is declared yet not initialized using an argument. By looking at the above program, you will notice that the *default constructor* is called for *quadx*. Take note that *quadx* is not constructed using empty parentheses. Actually, you cannot use empty parentheses to call default constructors.

Quadrilateral quadw;   // a default constructor will be called
Quadrilateral quadd ( );   // a default constructor will not be called

If you use empty parentheses, *quadd* will be considered as a function declaration and not an object declaration, which is what it is supposed to be. It will then be a function that returns a type *quadrilateral* value and does not take any arguments.

Uniform Initialization

In the above program, constructors were called by enclosing the arguments inside parentheses. This method is called the *functional form*. However, you do not always have to use the *functional form* when calling constructors. There are other syntaxes that you may find to be more appropriate for your program.

For instance, you may call constructors with single parameters using variable initialization syntax or an equal sign after the argument.

name_of_class name_of_object = value_of_initialization;

Recently, *uniform initialization* has been introduced. It is essentially the same as *functional form*, except that it uses braces instead of parentheses.

name_of_class name_of_object { value, value, ... }

Take a look at the following sample program. It features four ways on how to construct class objects whose constructors have single parameters.

```cpp
#include <iostream>
using namespace std;

class round
{
    double radius;
    public:
    round (double a)
    {
        radius = a;
    }
    double circumference ( )
    {
        return 2 * radius * 3.14;
    }
};

int main ( )
{
    round un (20.0);        // this is the functional form
    round deux = 30.0;      // this is the assignment initialization
    round trois = {40.0};   // this is the uniform initialization
    round quatre = {50.0};  // this is like plain old data type (POD)

    count << "The circumference is " << un.circumference ( ) << 'n';

    return 0;
```

```
}
```

If you run this program, you will get an output of:

The circumference is 125.6

The main advantage of preferring *uniform initialization* to *functional form* is the use of braces. If you use parentheses, you may confuse them with function declarations, but if you use braces, you will be able to see everything more clearly. You can also use braces to call default constructors explicitly.

Classes with Union and Struct

When it comes to defining classes, you do not have to limit yourself to the keyword *class*. In fact, you can also use the keywords *union* and *struct* to define classes.

Struct usually defines a variable or a structure type or a structure type. It is used to declare plain old data structures, but it can be used to declare classes with member functions as well. You can use *struct* as long as these member functions have the same syntax as *class*.

These two keywords are essentially the same, except that the class members declared using *struct* are publicly accessed by default. On the other hand, the class members declared using *class* are privately accessed by default.

Union is a special class type that holds only one non-static data member at a time. Its class specifier is similar to that of *struct* or *class*. The class members declared using *union* are publicly accessed by default.

Overloading Operators

Basically, classes define new types for C++. C++ types do not only use assignments and constructions when interacting with codes, but also operators. Here is an example of a basic operation:

```
int x, y, z;
x = y + z;
```

In the above example, different variable types are used. The addition and assignment operators are also used. How about a program with certain class types? Consider this example:

```
struct class
{
    string item;
    float price;
}
    x, y, z;
    x = y + z;
```

In the above example, the output of the addition operation on y and z is ambiguous. If you use this code, you will actually encounter a compilation error because your type *class* does not have any definite action for addition. Nonetheless, C++ will still let you overload operators so you can define their action for any type, such as classes.

Chapter 12 – Friends and Inheritance

What You Will Learn:

**Friend functions*

**Friend classes*

**Inheritance between classes*

**Derived and base classes*

**Inheritance and access control*

**Types of inheritance*

**Multiple inheritance*

Friend functions

The general rule is that protected and private class members are not accessible from outside the class wherein they are declared. Then again, this does not apply to *friends*. Non-member functions can access both the protected and private class members if they are declared as *friends* of that class. Such declaration is done by writing a declaration of the external function within the class and then including the *friend* keyword. Take a look at the following sample program:

#include <iostream>

```
using namespace std;

class quadrilateral
{
    int height, width;
    public:
    quadrilateral ( )
    {
    }
    quadrilateral (int w, int d) : height (w), width (d)
    {
    }
    int area ( )
    {
        return height * width;
    }
    friend quadrilateral duplicate (cost quadrilateral&);
};

quadrilateral duplicate (const quadrilateral& parameter)
{
    quadrilateral res;
    res.height = parameter.height * 2;
    rest.width = parameter.width * 2;
    return res;
}

int main ( )
{
    quadrilateral uno;
    quadrilateral dos (3, 4);
    uno = duplicate (dos);
    cout << uno.area ( ) << '\n';
    return 0;
}
```

If you run this program, your output will be:

48

The function *duplicate* is a *friend* of the class *quadrilateral*. Thus, *duplicate* can access the members *height* and *width*, which are both private, of the type *quadrilateral*. Looking closely at the program, what else have you noticed? Well, you should have seen that *duplicate* was never considered a class member neither in its declaration nor in its use in *main*. This is because duplicate is simply not a member of the class *quadrilateral*. Yes, it can access both the protected and private members, but it still remains a non-member. This only shows that even non-members have the ability to access protected and private members once they are declared as *friends*.

Friend Classes

Just like the function *friend*, the class *friend* is a class whose members can both access the protected and private members of a particular class. To help you understand friend classes further, consider and analyze the following program:

```
#include <iostream>
using namespace std;

class rhombus;
class quadrilateral
{
        int height, width;
        public:
```

```
        int area ( )
        {
                return (height * width);
        }
        void convert (rhombus w);
};

class rhombus
{
        friend class quadrilateral;
        private:
        int part;
        public:
        rhombus (int w) : part (w)
        {
        }
};

        void quadrilateral :: convert (rhombus w)
        {
                height = w.part;
                width = w.part;
        }

int main ( )
{
        quadrilateral quad;
        rhombus rho (4);
        quad.convert (rho);
        cout << quad.area ( );

        return 0;
}
```

If you run this program, you will get an output of:

16

In this program, the class *quadrilateral* is a *friend* of the class *rhombus*. Hence, the member functions of *quadrilateral* are allowed to access both the protected and the private members of *rhombus*. In addition, *quadrilateral* has access to the member variable *rhombus :: part*, which pertains to the sides of the rhombus.

If you will analyze the program carefully, you will notice that there is an empty class *rhombus* declaration at the start. You may think that this is not necessary, but it actually is. In fact, you need to have this declaration because the class *quadrilateral* uses *rhombus* and vice versa. *Quadrilateral* needs *rhombus* as a *convert* parameter while *rhombus* needs to declare *quadrilateral* as a *friend*.

It is important for you to remember that friendships are not corresponded until you specify them. In the sample program above, *quadrilateral* is considered as a *friend* by *rhombus*, but *rhombus* is not considered as a *friend* by *quadrilateral*. Thus, the member functions of *quadrilateral* have access to the private and protected members of *rhombus*, but the member functions of *rhombus* do not have access to the private and protected members of *quadrilateral*. Nevertheless, *rhombus* can also be declared as a friend of *quadrilateral* if necessary, so that it can have access to the other one's private and protected members.

Furthermore, you should keep in mind that friendships are not transitive. This means that a *friend* of a *friend* cannot be considered as a *friend* unless it is clearly specified in the program.

Inheritance

The concept of *inheritance* is amongst the most vital concepts in object-oriented programming. *Inheritance* is the process of creating new classes that retain the characteristics of the *base class*. It involves a *derived class* and a *base class*. The members of the *base class* are inherited by the *derived class*, which can also have its own members.

Inheritance lets you define a class in terms of another class. Hence, it can be easier for you to maintain and create an application. Also, this gives you a chance to reuse code functionality as well as take advantage of a speedy implementation time.

When you create a class, you can designate if a new class must inherit the members of another class. You can do this instead of creating entirely new member functions and data members, which can be more complex and time-consuming. The existing class is known as the *base class*, while the new class is known as the *derived class*.

Basically, inheritance provides the idea that there is an existing relationship between two classes. It is like saying that a fish is an animal and a salmon is a fish; therefore, a salmon is an animal.

Derived Class and Based Class

A certain class may be derived from at least one class. This means that it can inherit functions and data from numerous base classes. In order to define a derived class, you have to use a class derivation list and specify which one is the base class. A class derivation list contains the names of the base classes.

Inheritance and Access Control

A derived class can have access to any non-private member of the base class. Therefore, the members of the base class that are supposed to be inaccessible by the member functions of the derived class must be declared as private.

In summation, any class from within the same class can have access to all public, private, and protected members. Derived classes can have access to public and protected members, but not private members. Outside classes, on the other hand, can only have access to public members. They cannot access protected and private members.

Also, you have to remember that a derived class can inherit all the members in a base class, except for its:

- Copy constructors, constructors, and destructors
- Overload operators or assignment operators
- Friend functions
- Private members

Types of Inheritance

Base classes can be inherited through private, public, or protected inheritance. Of all the types of inheritance, public inheritance is the most common. Private and protected inheritances are actually rarely used. Anyway, when you use the different types of inheritance, see to it that you apply these rules:

- **For public inheritance**

    When you derive a class from a *public* base class, the *public* members of the base class turn into *public* members of the derived class, while the *protected* members of the base class turn into *protected* members of the derived class. The *private* members of a base class cannot be directly accessed from a derived class. However, they can still be accessed by calling the *protected* and *public* members of the base class.

- **For protected inheritance**

When you derive from a *protected* base class, the *protected* and the *public* members of the base class turn into *protected* members of the derived class.

- **For private inheritance**

When you derive from a *private* base class, the *protected* and the *public* members of the base class turn into *private* members of the derived class.

Multiple Inheritance

Classes may inherit from more than one class if they specify more base classes. When writing a program that involves multiple inheritance, see to it that you use commas to separate the base classes. For instance, if your program has a particular class for your *output*, yet you want your classes *quadrilateral* and *isosceles* to inherit its members as well, aside from the members of *geometry*, you can write the following code:

class quadrilateral: public geometry, public output;
class isosceles: public geometry, public output;

Conclusion

Thank you again for purchasing this book!

I hope this book was able to help you to learn and understand the C++ programming language!

The next step is to start from where you are now and try to learn something new. Keep in mind that you've only scratched the surface of all the things you can do in the world of C++!

Finally, if you enjoyed this book, please take the time to share your thoughts and post a review on Amazon. We do our best to reach out to readers and provide the best value we can. Your positive review will help us achieve that. It'd be greatly appreciated!

Thank you and good luck!

Check Out My Other Books

Below you'll find some of my other popular books that are popular on Amazon and Kindle as well. Simply click on the links below to check them out. Alternatively, you can visit my author page on Amazon to see other work done by me.

C Programming Success in a Day

Android Programming in a Day

Python Programming in a Day

PHP Programming Professional Made Easy

CSS Programming Professional Made Easy

Windows 8 Tips for Beginners

If the links do not work, for whatever reason, you can simply search for these titles on the Amazon website to find them.